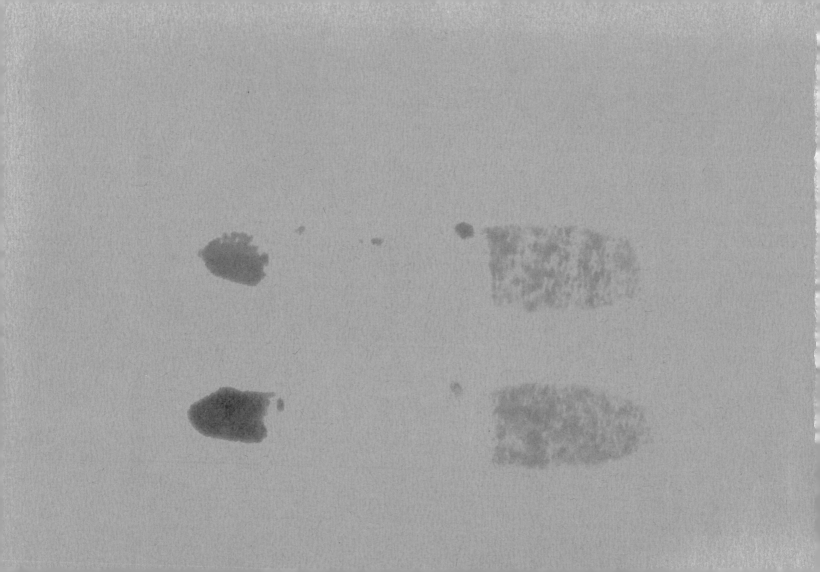

CHANUKAH

BY
HOWARD GREENFELD

DESIGNED
BY
BEA FEITLER

Holt, Rinehart and Winston
New York

Library of Congress Cataloging in Publication Data
Greenfeld, Howard.
  Chanukah.
   1. Hanukkah (Feast of lights)   I. Title.
BM695.H3G67   296.4'35   76-6527
ISBN 0-03-015566-5

CHANUKAH

Each year, in the month of December, Jews throughout the world celebrate the holiday of Chanukah. They light candles and play games and sing songs and eat festive meals. It is a joyous period that lasts eight days, during which Jews are reminded of their proud past, the memory of which gives them courage to live in the present and plan for the future—in spite of the periodic threats of oppression or even extermination that have been part of their history.

[6]

Chanukah celebrates a unique event, not only in Jewish history, but in the history of the world; it celebrates the first battles fought not for territory or material gains, but for the right to the free expression of a way of life—the right of religious freedom. Since that time, there have been many parallels, many struggles for human freedom on the part of many people. Today, perhaps even more then ever, we can learn a lesson from the stirring tale of a courageous and dedicated group of men who fought to preserve the religion, customs, and individuality of the Jewish people many centuries ago. It is a lesson for peoples everywhere who rightly feel the need to maintain and fight for their own identity. H.G.

 The early history of the Jews was that of a wandering, homeless people; not until the twelfth century B.C.E. (before the Common Era) did they have their own land. But even that land was almost constantly under the domination of foreign powers, to the point that Jews became unconcerned as to who ruled them, with one important condition: that they be allowed to live as Jews and follow the Laws of the Torah, the Laws of Moses. They had no cities or buildings or armies, but they had ideas and principles by which they had to live and for which

they were prepared to die. Willing to give up material possessions, they were nonetheless unwilling to surrender their faith and their individuality as Jews.

With this in mind, it is easy to understand the importance of the glorious victory of the Maccabees which is so joyously celebrated as the Festival of Chanukah.

Had it not been for one overambitious, angry king called Antiochus IV, there would have been no Maccabean Wars and no need for a Jewish armed resistance, for the Jews had lived peacefully under many rulers—Egyptian, Assyrian, Babylonian, Persian, and finally Greek. There had been many potential threats to Jewish existence, however, but none had

materialized, since the Jews were permitted to live as Jews. This
was even true under the reign of the Greek Alexander the
Great, who conquered much of the world, including Palestine,

the home of the Jews, in 333 B.C.E. Alexander's threat was a
powerful one, for it was more spiritual than military, his wish
being that all the conquered peoples become Greek, speak
the Greek language, worship the Greek gods, and in general

[12] think like Greeks. Since Greek civilization was rich in art and literature and philosophy as well as grace, most of the conquered peoples were charmed by its advantages and readily gave in.

Only the Jews, proud of their own values and identity, refused to give in. They resisted the influence of the Greeks. Alexander, anxious though he was to Hellenize (make Greek) all his lands, wisely permitted them to pursue their own ways.

Upon Alexander's death, his empire was divided into two kingdoms—Syria and Egypt. Palestine belonged first to Egypt and then to Syria. Though Hellenization was encouraged—and even accepted by a number of wealthy Jews who felt it was to

their advantage to do so — it was not imposed upon the con-
servative religious Jews. These latter steadfastly held to the
Laws of the Torah, kept the Sabbath, and refused to allow
idolatry to be practiced among them.

Then came the angry Antiochus, and with his rule a challenge
to Jewish existence. A ruthless, cruel man, he named himself
Antiochus Epiphanes, which means Antiochus the Divine; in
time, the Jews would call him Antiochus Epimanes — the Madman — and with good reason.

For this king, Hellenization was essential; all Jews had to
become Greek in every way. The wealthy Jews had already
become Greek in many ways, but under Antiochus they were

[14] prepared to help force Hellenization on those who opposed it. A moderate Jew was named high priest-governor of the Jews, a man who had shown his feelings by changing his name from

the Hebrew Joshua to the Greek Jason. He believed that it was in the best interest of all Jews to become part of the Greek culture. Under his rule Hellenization spread. So far as Jason was concerned, it was all right for Jews to remain Jews—it was to their own advantage, however, that they conduct themselves like Greeks and appear Greek. Seemingly, he was unaware that in this way all traces of Judaism would eventually disappear.

But Jason's attempts at compromise were not strong enough for Antiochus. Therefore, when a new war broke out, Antiochus saw an opportunity to replace Jason with a stronger man, one whose loyalty he could better count on in time of war. Jason's replacement was indeed stronger: his name was Menelaus, and he was determined to remove all differences between Greeks and Jews. Once again, the upper-class Jews agreed that it was more practical for the Jews to disappear

[16] within the community of the Greeks by becoming Hellenized.

 This time, however, things had gone too far. The devout Jews were enraged. Jason, too, was enraged. An active, if small, opposition arose. Their opportunity to act came when a rumor spread that Antiochus had been killed in a foreign war. An army of a thousand men, under the leadership of Jason, marched on Jerusalem, attempting to take control of the city and thus defeat the Hellenizers.

The rumor, however, proved to be false: Antiochus was alive. Outraged that even a small number of Jews had dared revolt, he summoned his huge army and put Jerusalem under the control of the military. The soldiers were ordered to kill all those Jews who showed the slightest sympathy to Antiochus's enemies. The edict was open to interpretation. Any Jew, as far as the soldiers were concerned, was sympathetic to the enemy. And they proceeded to carry out a senseless massacre of more than ten thousand Jews.

Mass slaughter of innocent people wasn't enough for Antiochus. In his fury he plundered the Temple, removing from it the gold altar, the lampstand, all the furniture, and the precious secret treasure as well.

The Jews went into deep mourning.

But the madman went even further. He was faced with threats

from the Egyptians and other foreign enemies. There was a need to strengthen his kingdom. He decided to strip the Jews—whose homeland was on the border with Egypt—of the very qualities that made them Jews. To achieve this, he issued the following decrees:

- All services in the Temple were to be halted.
- The Law of Moses by which all Jews lived was declared invalid.
- Observance of the Sabbath would be a capital offense.
- Circumcision was outlawed and offenders put to death.

Henceforth, all Jews were to worship the gods of the Greeks. Altars to these gods were to be built everywhere, and sacrifices were to be made to them—most often pigs and unclean cattle, both repugnant in the eyes of the Jews and prohibited to them by Jewish Law.

Antiochus was not threatening extermination of the Jewish people, but rather extermination of Judaism. For many, it meant the same thing.

As so often happens when a people are menaced, many Jews

[20] gave in, hoping by surrender to earn peace. But many others, more courageous and more devout, defied the angry ruler, disobeying his cruel decrees, though they knew that such disobedience would mean death.

Determined to root out all those who dared to go against his wishes, Antiochus sent his officers from town to town to enforce his laws, to see that the Jews were worshiping the Greek gods and eating the unclean meat. If a circumcised child was discovered, the mother was put to death, with her baby hanging around her neck. Whoever had performed the circumcision was slaughtered. The officers erected an altar in each town, and those who refused to worship at it were punished.

Antiochus would not rest until Judaism was destroyed.
But he did not realize that the Jews found strength in their beliefs and that many of them would continue to defy him.

One such man was an elderly priest, Matta-thias, who lived in the small village of Modin, on the road from Jerusalem to Jaffa. In him the Jews had found a leader. This the soldiers of Antiochus were to learn when they visited Modin in the winter of 166 B.C.E.

It was a routine visit. The soldiers set up an altar. By custom, they then asked who might be the most respected man in the village. The procedure was to ask such a man to set an example for the rest of the town. Told that he was Mattathias, the soldiers turned to him and promised that he and his five sons — Jochanan, Simon, Judah, Eleazar, and Jonathan — would be

richly rewarded if he were the first to carry out the orders of the king and worship at the newly built altar.

Riches, however, meant nothing to the pious and proud Mattathias. He answered firmly that he would never give in to the

king's decrees, that he and his sons would never worship at
that altar. The townspeople were stunned. One of them—in a
desire to win the favor of the soldiers—himself ran to the altar
and made the unholy sacrifice that was required to satisfy the
king's wishes. Mattathias angrily followed him and struck the
man down. In his fury he attacked the officer in charge and
killed him too. Thereupon, he tore down the altar and turned
to the townspeople:

"Let whoever is devoted to the Law follow me," he cried out.
And with that challenge, the old man and his sons fled to the
mountains. They disappeared.

They had settled in the wilderness, with other Jews who had

[24] found Jewish existence in the towns and cities too oppressive, who chose to live in poverty and hunger rather than to give up their ideals. They hoped by disappearing to live in peace.

Antiochus was not satisfied. The mere disappearance of these Jews was not enough for him. He ruthlessly sought them out. His ambition was to destroy each and every one of them. His task was made easier by the provision in Jewish Law that no

Jew could fight on the Sabbath. Antiochus's soldiers attacked on the Sabbath, slaughtering thousands of Jews who refused to fight back on that day.

For the Jews to survive, Mattathias had to compromise with the Law. He devised a new doctrine. Jews could not attack on the Sabbath, but they would be allowed to defend themselves at any time. It was a necessary compromise. With it, Antiochus and his men no longer found their task so easy.

The struggle in the mountains became more intense. Mattathias came to realize that his original goal—to fight for the right to live as a Jew—was not broad enough. It was his responsibility, and that of his followers, to put an end to the systematic destruction of Judaism throughout the entire land. Passive resistance had to become active resistance. The Jews had to fight back until the enemy restored the rights of all Jews to live as Jews.

To this end, they organized in small bands, going from village to village. They recruited other fighters. They also destroyed all that Antiochus's men had done. They tore down the idolatrous altars, they forcibly circumcised all the uncircumcised boys, and they compelled obedience to the Laws of the Torah. They demonstrated their intentions. They were even more determined to maintain Judaism than Antiochus was to destroy it.

The old Mattathias was a brave and wise leader. He fought for
freedom all his life.

 At his death, his son Judah took command. Judah was a worthy successor to his father. He swept down upon the enemy—both those Jews who disobeyed the Law and those who threatened Judaism—as a lion attacks his prey. He knew each hill and each valley and became a master of guerrilla warfare, attacking small villages and towns and relentlessly destroying the enemy.

Judah was soon famous everywhere for his skill and courage in battle. They called him Maccabee, which means hammer.

Those who fought with him were in time to become known as the Maccabees.

In the beginning, Judah and his men were almost ignored by

the government: they were considered of no more importance than a band of robbers. But as their successes grew and gave courage to others to join the Jewish resistance, Antiochus was forced to take notice. He sent his best generals in to defeat the small, stubborn band of Jewish fighters. But, one after another, these generals were themselves defeated. How, people wondered, could such a small, underequipped, and often underfed group of men conquer one mighty army after another? Where did they find their strength? For Judah, the answer was clear. Victory did not depend on the size of an army or the number of weapons it possessed but upon strength from heaven. The enemy was fighting to destroy, while the Jews were fighting for their freedom, their Law, and their right to worship their one God. It was these ideals that gave them the power to win battle after battle against the troops of the wrathful king.

[30] Antiochus grew desperate. Once and for all, he would crush and destroy the Maccabees. He summoned his greatest general, Lysias, and put him in charge of the army. Lysias, in turn, chose three generals, among them the famous Gorgias. He gave them forty thousand regular troops plus seven thousand horsemen, a force powerful enough to carry out the king's orders.

So it was that one day a seemingly invincible army led by Gorgias pitched camp at the plain of Emmaus, prepared for a final, destructive battle. When Judah's men saw them, they were struck with fear. But their leader gave them courage by telling them that God was on their side and that they could

conquer their fear by prayer and devotion. At Judah's sugges-
tion, they fasted, put on sackcloth and tore their clothes, con-
fessed all their sins, and prayed, renewing their allegiance to
God. Praying thus, their fears did indeed disappear.

On the eve of battle, the Maccabees were full of hope. Judah
appointed his officers and spoke to his soldiers, asking them to
be brave and reminding them that it would be better to die in
battle than to witness the destruction of Judaism.

As night fell and Judah was speaking to his men, General
Gorgias, at the enemy camp at Emmaus, was planning a surprise attack. Instead of waiting till morning, he would take
half his soldiers to destroy the sleeping Maccabees at their

encampment that very night.

Victory might have been his had not Judah learned of the plan. Feeling that his own chances of success had increased because Gorgias would be weakening his forces by dividing the army in half, he decided to launch an attack of his own. Under the cover of darkness, the courageous Judah led his army off to Emmaus, where he would find half of Gorgias' men. As for the arrival in the hills of the other half, Judah had made sure to leave burning fires in the camp so that Gorgias would not suspect that it was deserted. Judah's reputation as a master strategist who remembered every detail was well deserved.

Before dawn, the Maccabees arrived at the enemy camp.
They were but three thousand poorly equipped men against
a far greater number of superbly armed soldiers. But the ele-

ment of surprise was in their favor, as was a profound belief
in a God who would not fail them. While Gorgias's men slept,
the Maccabees sounded the trumpets, gave a great shout, and
attacked with the energy and determination of men inspired

[34] by the justness of their cause. The enemy, surprised and disoriented, were quickly overcome by Judah and his warriors and fled in total confusion.

In the meantime, Gorgias, finding the Maccabees' camp empty upon his arrival there during the night, was certain that the Jews had fled in terror. Triumphantly, he returned to Emmaus. To his own horror and that of his troops, he found nothing but the smoking ruin of their campsite. The general immediately realized that he had been outmaneuvered, and he and his army retreated. It was a brilliant tactical victory for Judah and the turning point in the Jews' struggle for freedom.

Antiochus, however, refused to give up. He would not accept

defeat at the hands of the Maccabees. It seemed to him im-
possible that this small band of men could defeat his mighty
forces.

The following year he sent Lysias himself, with a huge army,
into battle against the Jews. But once again Judah's inspired
soldiers routed the enemy against overwhelming odds. Lysias,
this time, had to concede that the Maccabees could never be
defeated, no matter how large and powerful an army was
mounted against them. He knew that they would rather die
than worship any god but their own, that they would never
give up their freedom, no matter what the price. Such a spirit
was truly invincible.

[36] The news of the total defeat of his troops was conveyed to Antiochus. Humiliated and desperate, the once-mighty king fled to the coast. On his way, he was mocked and jeered at by his own people. In shame, he threw himself into the sea and drowned.

Judaism had survived, and for Judah the Maccabee, triumph meant, most importantly, purification of the Temple, which had been profaned. He appointed priests who had never abandoned their faith to perform this task. Unclean stones were removed, the idols were thrown out, and the impure altar was destroyed. A new altar was lovingly built out of whole stone; new holy

dishes were made; and an altar of incense, a table for loaves of bread, and a golden seven-branched candlestick were brought into the cleansed Temple. Then the loaves of bread were

placed on the table, and new curtains were hung.
The House of God had been purified.
On the twenty-fifth day of the month of Kislev (the ninth month of the Hebrew year), the Temple was joyfully rededi-

cated. It was three years to the day since the first pagan sacrifice had been offered upon the altar. There had been three years of hardship and suffering, but none doubted that it had been worth the struggle. There was singing and chanting. The people fell on their faces to thank heaven, and Judah lighted the lamps of the menorah. There was but one cruse of undefiled oil left for the ceremony (the Greeks had unpurified the rest of the oil three years before), just enough to last one day. Miraculously, the oil lasted for eight days, the entire period of the rededication ceremony.

In commemoration of this great event, Judah the Maccabee decreed that each year, for eight days beginning with the

twenty-fifth day of Kislev, the rededication of the Temple
should be observed with gladness and joy. It was to be called
the Festival of Rededication (Chanukah) or the Festival of

Lights. And since that time, every year and in every part of
the world in which Jews live, it has been so celebrated. Since
the time of Antiochus, other men and other nations have tried
to destroy Judaism, but none has ever succeeded.